Beauregard& Me

and selected poems

by David Yarbrough

Illustrations by
Bruce Dupree

Beauregard& Me and selected poems

by
David Yarbrough

Illustrations by
Bruce Dupree

UNIVERSITY OF LOUISIANA AT LAFAYETTE PRESS

for Rene

© 2021 by University of Louisiana at Lafayette Press
All rights reserved
ISBN 13 (paper): 978-1-946160-75-1

http://ulpress.org
University of Louisiana at Lafayette Press
P.O. Box 43558
Lafayette, LA 70504-3558

Printed on acid-free paper in the United States
Library of Congress Cataloging-in-Publication Data

Names: Yarbrough, David 1959- author. | Dupree, Bruce, illustrator.
Title: Beauregard & me : and selected poems / by David Yarbrough ;
    illustrations by Bruce Dupree.
Other titles: Beauregard and me
Description: Lafayette, LA : University of Louisiana at Lafayette Press,
    2021. | Audience: Ages 4-8.
Identifiers: LCCN 2021005432 | ISBN 9781946160751 (hardcover)
Subjects: LCSH: Children's poetry, American. | LCGFT: Poetry.
Classification: LCC PS3625.A723 B43 2021 | DDC 811/.6--dc23
LC record available at https://lccn.loc.gov/2021005432

Beauregard & Me and selected poems is a work of fiction. Names, characters, and places are either the product of the
author's imagination or used fictitiously. Any resemblance to local persons, living or dead is entirely coincidental.

Table of Contents

Beauregard & Me

The noises at night
Scare Beauregard, my bear.
He hears clinking and clanging
And sees ghosts that aren't there.
I hold him real close
And tell him he's safe.
But I still know he's frightened
By the look on his face.
When I say that I love him,
He sleeps with a smile.
He knows he's OK
And his life is worthwhile.
But there's still one thing,
I can't tell my bear.
While he's sleeping, I'm frightened
'Cause the noises are there.

I Had My Picture Taken

They dressed me up
And combed my hair.
Said, "Please sit still"
In that uncomfortable chair.
Smile real big,
Not your usual frown.
Look straight at the camera.
No, please don't look down.
Don't squirm. Now look up.
Don't mess up your clothes.
Now isn't this fun?
Oh, don't pick your nose!
They finished my picture.
I said, "Let me see."
Well, she's a cute little girl,
But that just isn't me.

Talking with a Goldfish

I can tell my goldfish secrets.
He always keeps his word
Never, till his dying day,
To pass on what he's heard.
I can tell him that I don't like school,
I just don't want to go.
I tell him that I like some girls,
And no one has to know.
I try to tell him everything,
All that I feel and see.
I wish that he could talk some too
And share some things with me.

Little Steps

My little friend takes little steps
On little feet, in little shoes.
His little world has lots of room
With lots of little things to do.
His little face has a little smile.
His little voice sounds glad.
I wish that I was little too,
'Cause grown-ups make me mad.

A Friend

A friend is one who holds your hand,
Holds you close and understands,
Helps you see there are no ghosts,
And loves you when you need it most.
To have a friend is really fine,
And I'm so glad that you are mine.

Housework

Bang!
Clang!
Bump and break.
All the noises that I make.
Crash!
Bash!
Scrape and boom.
When I'm cleaning up my room.
Clomp!
Stomp!
I do confess,
If I make a bigger mess,
Mom will tell me, "Go and play,
Clean your room another day."

Grow

Grow, grow, grow.
I grow out of my clothes.
My mother says I grow so fast.
I think I grow too slow.

5

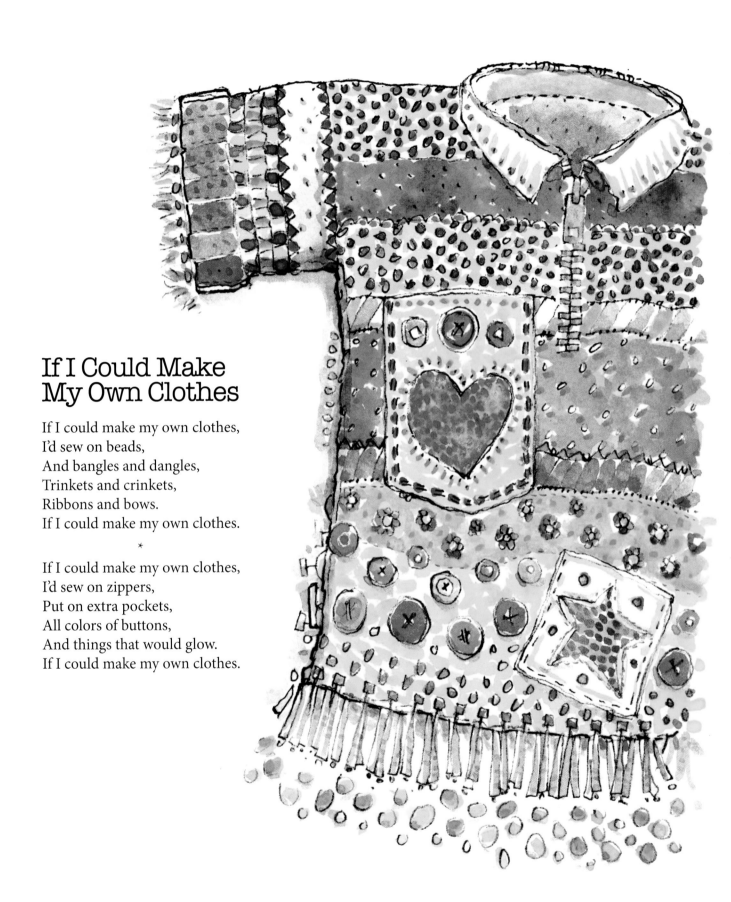

If I Could Make My Own Clothes

If I could make my own clothes,
I'd sew on beads,
And bangles and dangles,
Trinkets and crinkets,
Ribbons and bows.
If I could make my own clothes.

*

If I could make my own clothes,
I'd sew on zippers,
Put on extra pockets,
All colors of buttons,
And things that would glow.
If I could make my own clothes.

6

A Wallawat

There he goes,
Right by your nose.
I just saw a Wallawat.
Big and green with purple spots,
Yellow hair and big blue feet,
Bright red wings and orange teeth.
Wallawats are rare they say.
You just don't see them much today.
But I just did.
Well, think of that.
A Wallawat, right where we're at.
A Wallawat, oh, golly gee,
I hope he doesn't land on me.

Bubble Bath

Bubbles, bubbles, bubbles.
Bubbles everywhere.
Bubbles on my arms and legs,
Bubbles in my hair.
Bubbles, bubbles on my toes,
Bubbles going up my nose.
Bubbles on my hands and feet,
Bubble baths are really neat.
I know it always works for me.
Just try it once, I think you'll see.
It's hard to feel real sad and blue
When bubbles are all over you.

Some Things
Are Hard to Hear

What's that you say?
I haven't heard.
I haven't heard a single word.
Speak up, please,
Loud and clear.
Louder still,
I just can't hear
With this banana in my ear.

Dad Bought Tires
at a Flea Market

Bumpity, clumpity, clumpity, clump,
This ride is not a soft one.
Clumpity, clumpity, bumpity, bump,
I wish we kept the old ones.
Bumpity, clump, clumpity, bump,
Riding in this car,
Clumpity, clump, bumpity, bump,
We surely won't get far.
Bumpity, bumpity, bumpity, bump,
I don't think I agree,
Clumpity, clumpity, clumpity, clump,
Square tires are for me
(Even if they're free).

The Wall

There's a wall in my room that's nothing but white.
No pictures or windows from ceiling to floor,
I don't need that stuff,
I see so much more.
If I want to go sail, I feel wind and waves.
I'm out on the ocean with mean Captain Hook,
There are no pictures.
All I do is look.
Now I'm galloping fast with Billy the Kid.
I'm up on a horse on the wide open plain,
I'm out robbing banks,
Or hopping a train.
Now I'm a fireman or maybe police.
I smile while thinking of the people I'll meet.
They're kings and they're queens,
Or people like me.
People who play,
Look at walls and can see
All of the things that
Someday they will be.

The Animal's Home

An otter oughta live in water,
Simply 'cause it rhymes.
Up in trees?
Why, bumble bees
And chimpanzees that swing with ease.
Dogs and hogs,
In hollow logs.
And all the bears,
Just anywhere.
For me,
I'll live in Tennessee.
What rhymes with you?

Santa's Sack

Oreos or sugar cookies,
Chocolate chip or ice cream cones?
If I don't pick just what he likes,
He might pass by my home.
Maybe this, or how 'bout that?
One of these, and these, and those,
And this would surely warm his toes.
I hope I've picked the perfect snack
To bribe a gift from Santa's sack.

Stomping

Stomp, stomp, stomp.
I stomp around my room.
Stomping is like walking bad,
I do it when I get real mad.
Clomp, clomp, clomp.
The sound of stomps on stairs.
I clomp until my face turns red.
I clomp up stairs and 'round my bed.
Stomp, stomp, stomp.
Sometimes I close my eyes
And pretend I'm stomping hard and bad
On what it was that made me mad.
Stomp, clomp, crash!
Uh-oh, an extra noise.
I turn and look,
And then I see
I stomped a gift Dad gave to me.

(Maybe I'll try to quit stomping.)

Animal Crackers

I was hunting for animals deep in my room.
I spied a white tiger and then a baboon.
An elephant perched on the end of my bed.
I held up a lion, way over my head.
A kangaroo jumped and almost got loose,
But he tripped and fell after hitting a moose.
I caught all of these creatures,
And then one by one,
I ate them, I did,
I ate every one.
The lion and tiger, the moose and baboon,
I ate every one without leaving my room.
I filled up my tummy,
Then started to think,
After eating those cookies
I sure want a drink.

The Land of Crazy Animals

There's a land of crazy animals
I really want to see.
There's monkeeroos and giratamus
And great big elephanteeze.
There's dats and cogs
And cute cowfrogs.
At night they howl at the moon.
There's a land of crazy animals,
I hope to go there soon.

*

There's a land of crazy animals,
Where everything's so strange.
The bullfish live way up in trees,
And horseflies roam the range.
There's rickens and hules, and
I heard there were mules
That will eat right out of your hand.
It seems like such fun, so tonight I will run
To the crazy animal land.

Dum Diddle Dee
and Dum Diddle Doo

Dum Diddle Dee and Dum Diddle Doo,
Two people,
Two people,
Just like me and you.
Dum Diddle Dee and Dum Diddle Doo,
They would laugh
And would cry
And know what to do.
They cleaned up their rooms and they played in the sun.
They loved,
And they laughed
And showed everyone,
That Dum Diddle Doo and Dum Diddle Dee,
Could grow old,
And stay young,
And love just to be,
Mister Dum Diddle Doo and Miss Dum Diddle Dee,
Two people,
Two people,
Just like you and me.

When I Was Just a Little Kid

When I was just a little kid,
A little, little, little kid,
I only asked one question,
I really, really did.
I asked a million people,
Minus one or two.
But none of them could answer me.
I guess that no one knew.
The question's not a hard one.
The answer might be though.
Why aren't there any special clothes
To cover up my nose?

Candy Clothes

Every town should have a bailor,
A man who bakes and is also a tailor.
He'd bake the most delicious clothes
To cover your head and cover your toes.
Chocolate socks and shirts made of cake,
Blueberry jeans, now that's what he'd make.
A suit made of muffins and licorice shoes—
They'd never get dirty. (They'd hardly get used.)
Dresses of peppermint or soft caramel,
A banana split bonnet that would taste oh so swell.
Just think of the time that you won't have to spend
Washing your clothes just to wear them again.
While getting undressed for bed late at night,
You could lay out your clothes on the table, just right.
Your mom would come in, and then count one, two, three,
On your mark, get set, there's your clothes,
Now let's eat!

I Used to Be the Baby

I used to be the baby,
The one that they would hold.
It didn't seem so long ago,
But now I feel so old.

*

I was the one they played with,
We'd run and hide and seek.
But now when I go off to hide,
They don't come look for me.

*

They have a brand new baby,
A bouncing baby boy.
He'll likely take up all their time
And break my favorite toys.

*

I used to be the baby,
The one they like to see.
But now they have another boy.
Do they still care for me?

Herman Dean

My turtle's name is Herman Dean.
His feet are webbed, his shell is green.
His bowl is clean, he's not real loud.
I love him lots, he makes me proud.
Herman listens when I talk,
Sometimes I take him when I walk.
Herman Dean got sick one day.
He closed his eyes and wouldn't play.
My mother said that Herman's dead.
"That happens to all things," she said.
Why did Herman close his eyes?
Did I do something to make him die?
My mom says I am not to blame,
All living things are just the same.
Like plants and flowers, birds and bees,
Cats and dogs, and even trees.
There is a time when things just die.
They go to heaven in the sky.
I liked when Herman was with me,
Now that he's gone, I think I see
That even though he's far away,
He still remembers when we'd play.
So do I.

Caterpillars

Caterpillars climb in trees,
Walking on a hundred knees.
They climb real high and make a home.
Away from it, they never roam.
They wait inside a real long time.
(Longer than I could wait in mine.)
They wait and wait, it seems so strange.
Then slowly, they begin to change.
After enough time goes by,
They change into a butterfly.

I Wish

I wish, I wish, I wish
That dinner was chocolate cake.
I'd clean my plate and ask for more
(But get a stomachache).
I wish, I wish, I wish
There wasn't any school.
I'd stay at home and play all day,
Not worrying 'bout the rules.
I wish, I wish, I wish
I could stay up all night long.
I wouldn't have to go to bed.
Now what could be so wrong?
I wish, I wish, I wish.
Oh, wishes don't come true.
I guess that I'll just go to sleep,
'Cause in dreams, they sometimes do.

The Day That Almost Was

We almost went to the park
To run and hide,
Slip and slide,
Crawl and play
The day away.
We almost went to the park.

*

We almost went to the pool
To jump and swim,
And dive right in,
Lay out in
The sun so warm.
We almost went to the pool.

*

We almost did a lot,
Like run and play
The entire day.
But now with rain,
It's such a pain.
The day that almost was.

Daydreaming

Stretch out on the ground
And look up at the clouds.
What do you see?
What could it be?
A herd of horses running fast,
A pirate ship that's sailing past,
A circus with lions and clowns.
They smile at you while looking down.
Or maybe all of the clouds so white
Are snowcapped mountains, glistening bright.
Sometimes they look like flowers to me
Or giant waves out on the sea.
I'd like to spend a day or two
Just looking at the clouds with you.

Sheets

Turned up, turned down,
Slip inside and kick around.
Pull them up close to my chin
Or bunch 'em up down at the end.
They warm my feet and hide my face,
Tucked in real tight or out of place.
Pulled up like a tall teepee,
Crawl inside and let them hide me.
What makes my bed a place so neat
Are all the things I do with sheets.

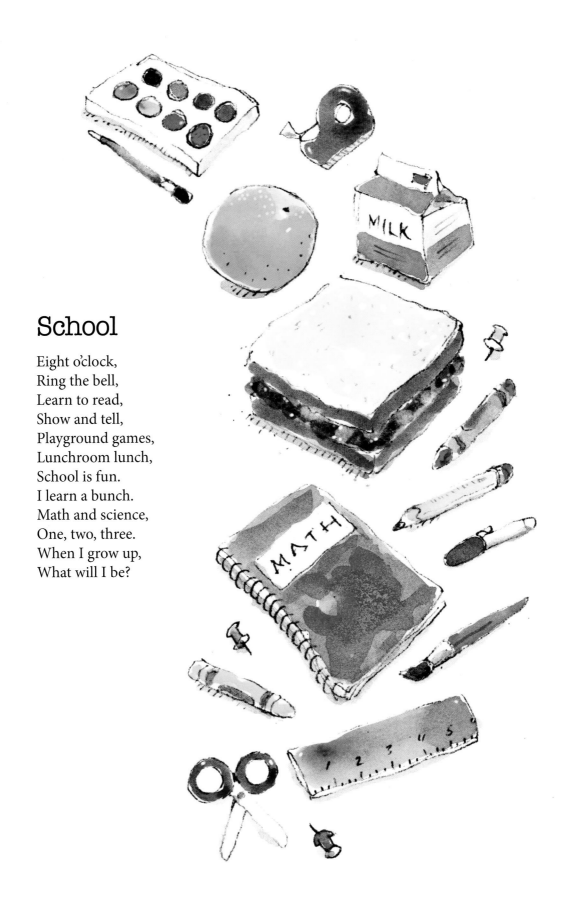

School

Eight o'clock,
Ring the bell,
Learn to read,
Show and tell,
Playground games,
Lunchroom lunch,
School is fun.
I learn a bunch.
Math and science,
One, two, three.
When I grow up,
What will I be?

Hug

Sometimes when I feel real bad,
I give a hug,
It makes me glad.
Even if I feel OK,
I give a hug,
It helps my day.
If I see my sister frown,
I give a hug,
It turns around.
Need a hug? Just ask, it's free,
And it's OK
If you hug me.

Dessert

Hamburgers, French fries,
Some corn and peas,
Pass me the carrots,
I'll have more, please.
Yes, I'll have salad,
Green beans? OK.
Not that I like 'em,
But I'll eat 'em today.
I eat and I eat,
Eat really fast.
Just got to finish,
'Cause dessert's last.
I drink all my milk,
Clean off my plate.
The good part is here,
I don't want to wait.
I'm done with dinner.
What's coming last?
Broccoli pudding!
I think I'll pass.

My Room

I'm not gonna pick up my clothes.
I'll throw and I'll toss them
And stack them so high
That no one will ever get by.
I won't put away all my toys.
They're scattered around me,
All over the floor.
You can't even open the door.
I'm not gonna clean up my room.
Wait—I might have to,
Just like my mom said.
Now it's night, and where is my bed?

A Day at the Zoo

The elephant's nose,
Is long like a hose,
And monkeys, they swing in the trees.
The birds and the snakes
Live close to the lake.
The giraffe is the tallest I've seen.
There's the fat hippopotamus
Who smiles at all of us.
I wonder if he's thinking of lunch.
The tigers will growl,
The leopards will prowl,
The lion's roar scares me a bunch.
There's soft furry deer
That let me get near.
I like them, and they like me too.
My day sure was fun,
I saw every one
Of the animals here at the zoo.

***

A Dream I'd Like to Share

I dreamed that I was flying,
Floating high above the ground.
I could see my room,
I spotted the moon,
And no one else was around.

I dreamed that I was swimming,
Like a fish through ocean blue.
It felt safe and warm,
Swimming under storms.
I'd like swimming there with you.

I dreamed that I was running.
I was fastest in the race.
Ran quick by the trees,
So fast like a breeze,
A big smile was on my face.

I dreamed we were together,
Walking slowly on the sand.
Your hand was in mine
For such a long time.
I'd like to live in that land.